Who's in my family tree?

Mike Jackson

Illustrated by Diana Bowles

First published in this edition in 2011 by
Evans Publishing Group
2A Portman Mansions
Chiltern Street
London W1U 6NR

www.evansbooks.co.uk

British Library Cataloguing in Publication Data:
A CIP catalogue record for this book is available from the British Library

ISBN: 9780237544898

Planned and produced by Discovery Books
Cover designed by Rebecca Fox

For permission to reproduce copyright material the author and publishers gratefully acknowledge the following: Beamish, the North of England Open Air Museum: pages 7, 9, 21; istock: cover; Robert Harding Picture Library: page 27; The Hulton Deutsch Collection: pages 10, 17, 19, 23, 24

Printed by Great Wall Printing Company in Chai Wan, Hong Kong,
August 2011, Job Number 1672.

CONTENTS

We're looking through the things in Grandma Betty's attic.
Let's see what's in this old photo album!

Have a look but be careful – some of the photos in there are very old!

Who's that, Grandma?

That's your Great-great-great-grandpa Samuel. That picture was taken about one hundred and fifteen years ago.

Can you see him fixing a shoe to a horse's hoof? He was a blacksmith, just like his father. Samuel was married to Agatha, so she is your great-great-great-grandma.

Who are these three girls wearing hats?

They are your Great-great-grandma Maud, and her two sisters, Ethel and Martha.

Martha met an American soldier during the First World War. After the war she married him and went to live in America. I think her husband became a farmer.

No, Ethel died when she was only 19. People often died young in those days because there was no proper medicine.

Let's take the albums downstairs and I'll draw you a family tree.

It's a diagram that shows where everybody fits into a family. It has dates so that you know when somebody was born and when they died.

Here is the first part of our family tree.

Your Great-great-grandma Maud had two other brothers and two other sisters. Their names were Theodore, Wilfred, Kathleen and Harriet.

People often had big families in those days.

Maud married Stanley and they had three children — Winifred, Arthur and Edith. Winifred was your Great-grandma.

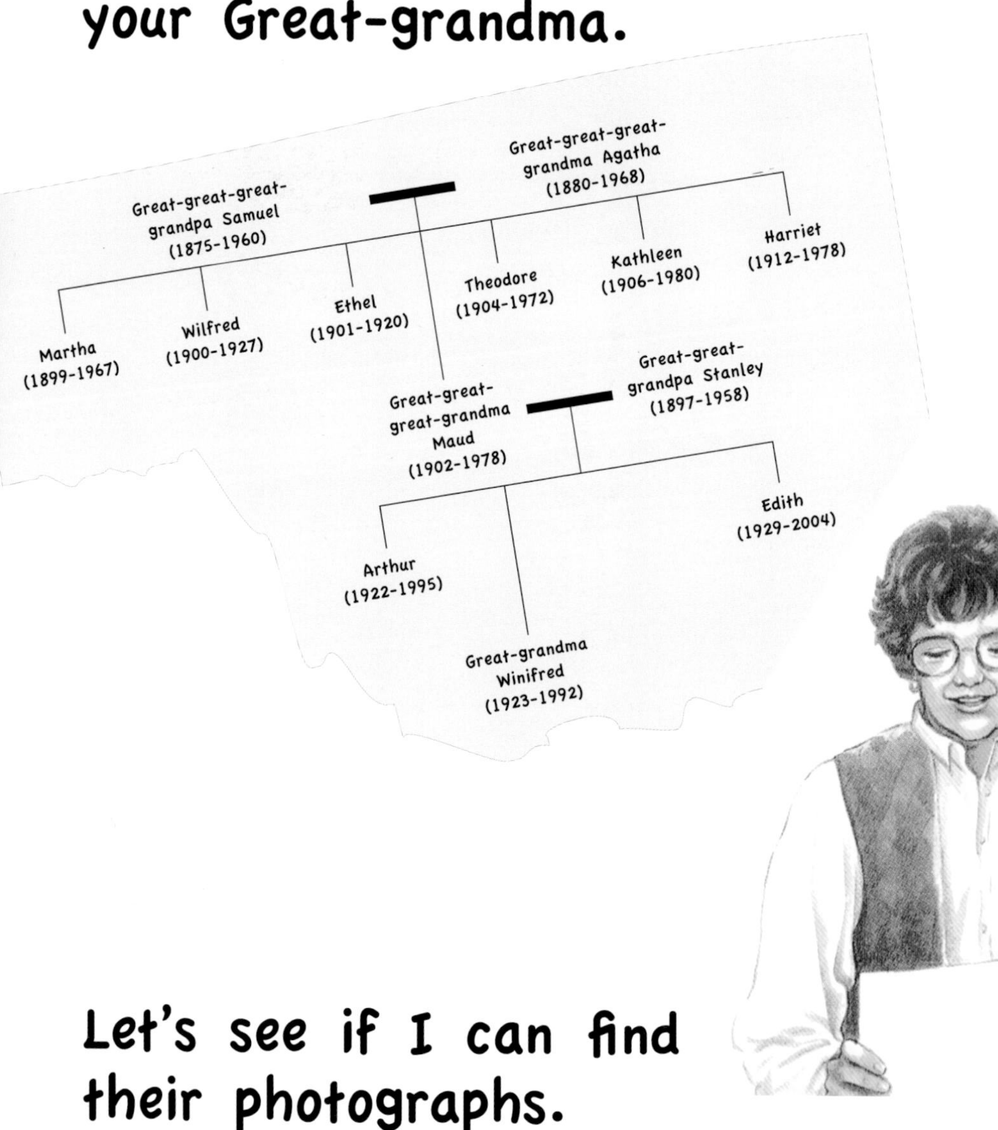

Let's see if I can find their photographs.

Yes, that is your Great-grandma Winifred. She was my mother.

And here is your Great-grandpa, my father. His name was Frank.

He was a train driver. In those days trains were powered by steam. Here's another picture of him in his cab.

Who do you think this baby is?

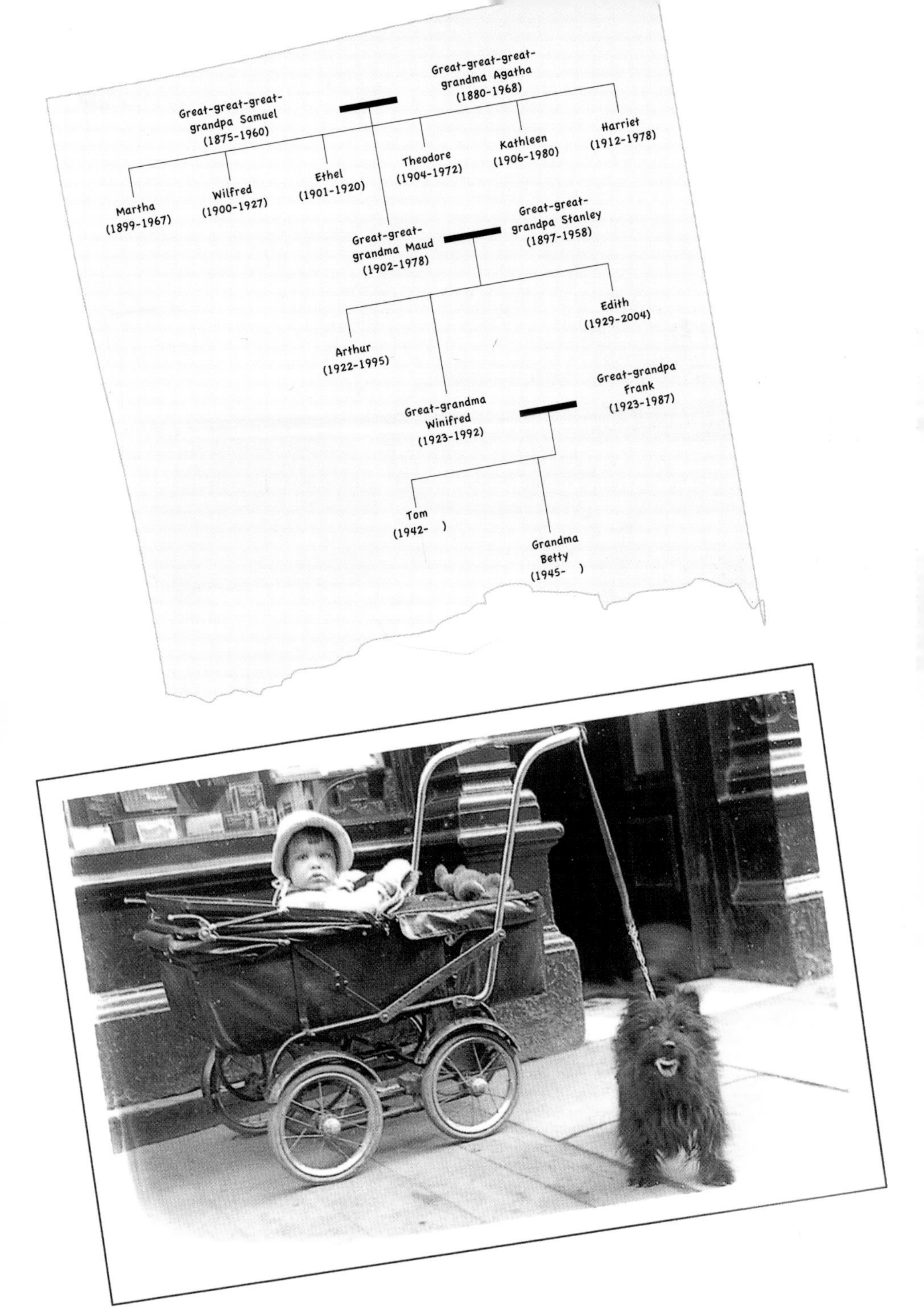

Great-great-great-grandpa Samuel (1875-1960)
Great-great-great-grandma Agatha (1880-1968)
Martha (1899-1967)
Wilfred (1900-1927)
Ethel (1901-1920)
Theodore (1904-1972)
Kathleen (1906-1980)
Harriet (1912-1978)
Great-great-grandma Maud (1902-1978)
Great-great-grandpa Stanley (1897-1958)
Arthur (1922-1995)
Edith (1929-2004)
Great-grandma Winifred (1923-1992)
Great-grandpa Frank (1923-1987)
Tom (1942-)
Grandma Betty (1945-)

Is this another picture of you, Grandma?

No, that's my brother Tom saying goodbye to my father.

My father joined the army and fought in the Second World War.

Here's a picture of your Grandpa Sidney and me on our wedding day.

That was over forty years ago.

He was a shipbuilder. There aren't many shipbuilders left in this country today.

I bet you can't guess who this is!

Yes. We often took holidays by the sea when your mother and Paul were children.

Now our family tree is nearly finished, but who's missing?

That's right. We'll put your names at the bottom – Tom, Kelly and Tammy.

You could draw another family tree showing your dad's side of the family. I expect Grandpa Peter has lots of old pictures you could look at, too.

Fun activities

Here is Tom, Kelly and Tammy's family tree, but some of the names are missing. Can you fill in the gaps? Look back through the book to help you.

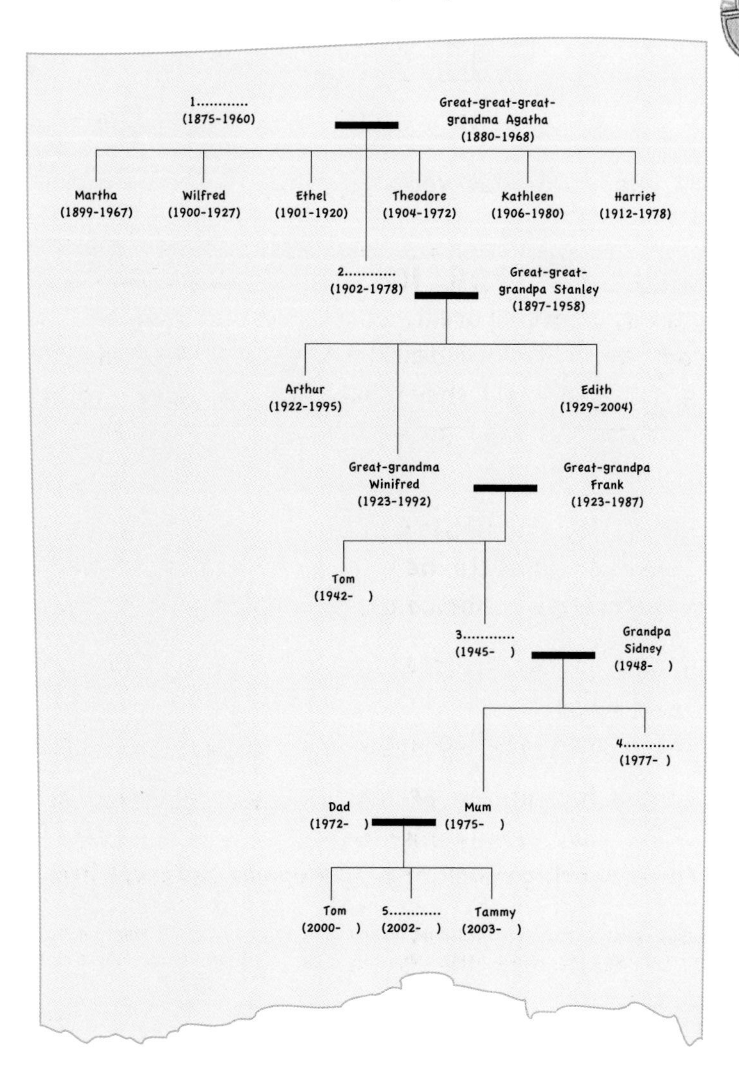

Answers: 1. Great-great-great grandpa Samuel, 2. Great-great grandma Maud, 3. Grandma Betty, 4. Uncle Paul, 5. Kelly

Copy the timeline below and see if you can match the following events to the correct date. We've entered one to start you off. The answers are at the bottom of the page.

Great-great grandma Maud was born
Great-grandma Winifred died
Edith died
Grandma Betty was born
Tom, Kelly and Tammy's mum was born

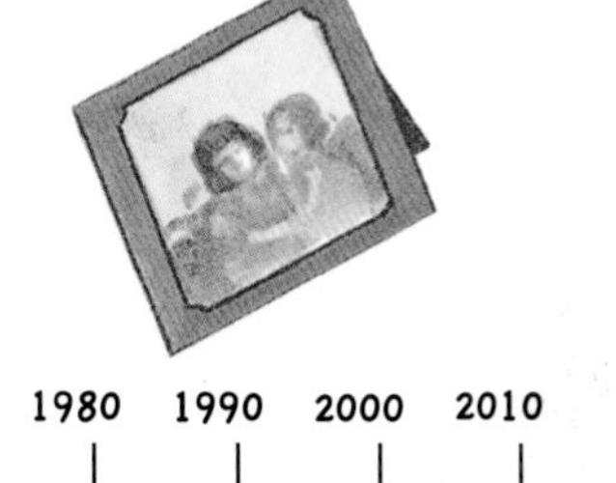

1900 1910 1920 1930 1940 1950 1960 1970 1980 1990 2000 2010

1902 1939 1965 1992 2004 Edith died

Can add the year that you were born to the timeline, too?

Talk to someone in your family – it could be a parent, a grandparent, aunt or uncle. Find out about their childhood. Write a story describing what it was like for them growing up. Where did they live? Did they have brothers or sisters? Where did they go to school? What did their parents do?

Interesting websites:

A step-by-step guide to help you start tracing your own family history: http://www.bbc.co.uk/history/familyhistory/

You can use the craft ideas on this site to help you to create your own family tree:
http://www.enchantedlearning.com/crafts/familytree/

This website has plenty of tips if you're thinking of researching your family history:
http://www.worldgenweb.org/%7Ewgw4kids/start.htm

Answers:
1902: Great-great grandma Maud was born 1939: Grandma Betty was born 1965: Tom, Kelly and Tammy's mum was born 1992: Great-grandma Winifred died 2004: Edith died

Index